Glory to God in the highest, and on earth peace, go ...
Luke 2:14

_ _ _ _ _ to God in the _ _ _ _ _ _ _, and on earth _ _ _ _ _,
goodwill _ _ _ _ _ _ men. Luke 2:14

The child grew and became strong in spirit, filled with wisdom;
and the grace of God was upon him. Luke 2:40

The _ _ _ _ _ grew and became _ _ _ _ _ _ _ in spirit, filled
with _ _ _ _ _ _; and the _ _ _ _ _ of God was
_ _ _ _ him. Luke 2:40

When the sun was setting, all those who had any that were sick ... brought them to him and he ... healed them. Luke 4:40

When the sun was _ _ _ _ _ _ _ , all _ _ _ _ _ who had any that were _ _ _ _ ... brought them to him and he ... _ _ _ _ _ _ them. Luke 4:40

He got into one of the boats ... then he sat down and taught
the multitudes from the boat. Luke 5:3

_ _ got into one of the _ _ _ _ _ ... then he sat down and
_ _ _ _ _ _ the _ _ _ _ _ _ _ _ _ from the _ _ _ _. Luke 5:3

Whoever hears my sayings and does them ... is like a man building a house, who dug deep and laid the foundation on the rock. Luke 6:47-48

Whoever _ _ _ _ _ _ my _ _ _ _ _ _ _ _ and does them ... is like a man _ _ _ _ _ _ _ _ _ a house, who dug _ _ _ _ and laid the foundation on the rock. Luke 6:47-48

He said to the woman, 'Your faith has saved you. Go in peace.' Luke 7:50

He said to the _ _ _ _ _, 'Your _ _ _ _ _ has _ _ _ _ _ you.
Go in _ _ _ _ _.' Luke 7:50

Jesus said, 'Foxes have holes and birds of the air have nests, but the Son of Man has nowhere to lay his head.' Luke 9:58

Jesus said, ' _ _ _ _ _ have holes and _ _ _ _ _ of the air have _ _ _ _ _ _, but the _ _ _ of Man has _ _ _ _ _ _ _ _ to lay his head.' Luke 9:58

If you then, being evil, know how to give good gifts to your children, how much more will your heavenly Father give the Holy Spirit to those who ask him. Luke 11:13

If you then, _ _ _ _ _ evil, know how to give good _ _ _ _ _ to your children, how much more will your heavenly Father give the _ _ _ _ Spirit to those who ask him. Luke 11:13

Are not five sparrows sold for two copper coins? And not one of them is forgotten before God. Luke 12:6

Are not five _ _ _ _ _ _ _ _ sold for two _ _ _ _ _ _ coins?
And not one of them is _ _ _ _ _ _ _ _ _ before God.
Luke 12:6

Consider the lilies, how they grow. They neither toil nor spin; and yet I say to you, even Solomon in all his glory was not arrayed like one of these. Luke 12:27

_ _ _ _ _ _ _ _ the lilies, how they grow. They neither _ _ _ _nor spin; and yet I say to you, even _ _ _ _ _ _ _ in all his glory was not arrayed like one of these. Luke 12:27

He calls together his friends and neighbours saying, 'Rejoice with me, for I have found my sheep which was lost.' Luke 15:6

He calls _ _ _ _ _ _ _ _ his friends and _ _ _ _ _ _ _ _ _ _ _ saying, '_ _ _ _ _ _ _ with me, for I have found my sheep which was lost.' Luke 15:6

God be merciful to me a sinner. Luke 18:13

God be _ _ _ _ _ _ _ _ to me a _ _ _ _ _ _. Luke 18:13

Zacchaeus ran ahead and climbed up into a
sycamore tree to see Jesus. Luke 19:4

_ _ _ _ _ _ _ _ _ _ ran ahead and climbed up into a
_ _ _ _ _ _ _ _ _ tree to see _ _ _ _ _. Luke 19:4

Jesus said, 'Father forgive them, for they do not know what they do.'
Luke 23:34

Jesus said, 'Father _ _ _ _ _ _ _ them, for _ _ _ _ do not know what they do.' Luke 23:34

'Abide with us, for it is toward evening...' And Jesus went in to stay with them. Luke 24:29

'_ _ _ _ _ with us, for it is _ _ _ _ _ _ evening...' And Jesus went in to _ _ _ _ with them. Luke 24:29

He taught the people in the temple and preached the gospel.
Luke 20:1

He _ _ _ _ _ _ _ the people in the _ _ _ _ _ _ and
_ _ _ _ _ _ _ _ _ the gospel. Luke 20:1